DINOSAURS

TRICERATOPS

BY STEPH GIEDD

An Imprint of Abdo Publishing
abdobooks.com

abdobooks.com

Published by Abdo Publishing, a division of ABDO, PO Box 398166, Minneapolis, Minnesota 55439.

Printed in the United States of America, North Mankato, Minnesota.
102023
012024

Cover Photo: iStockphoto
Interior Photos: Vladimir Bolokh/Shutterstock Images, 4–5; Shutterstock Images, 7, 12–13, 17 (*Triceratops*), 17 (elephant), 17 (scale), 18; Hadrani Hasan/Shutterstock Images, 9; Bettmann/Getty Images, 10; Aurelien Meunier/Getty Images News/Getty Images, 14; Lukas Krbec/Shutterstock Images, 20–21; Pier Marco Tacca/Getty Images News/Getty Images, 23, 25; Universal Pictures/Moviepix/Getty Images, 26; Freestyle Images/Shutterstock Images, 28–29

Editor: Marley Richmond
Series Designer: Mary Shaw

Library of Congress Control Number: 2023939629

Publisher's Cataloging-in-Publication Data

Names: Giedd, Steph, author.
Title: Triceratops / by Steph Giedd
Description: Minneapolis, Minnesota: Abdo Publishing, 2024 | Series: Dinosaurs | Includes online resources and index.
Identifiers: ISBN 9781098292706 (lib. bdg.) | ISBN 9798384910640 (ebook)
Subjects: LCSH: Dinosaurs--Juvenile literature. | Prehistoric animals--Juvenile literature. | Triceratops--Juvenile literature.
Classification: DDC 567.90--dc23

CONTENTS

Triceratops was a type of dinosaur called a ceratopsian. Ceratopsians had many similar features, such as head frills.

CHAPTER 1

TOP TRICERATOPS

A three-horned dinosaur noses through shrubs and bushes. The *Triceratops* (treye-SEH-ruh-tahps) moves slowly. He looks for plants to eat. He seems to be eating alone. Most *Triceratops* do. But that can be dangerous.

Without a **herd**, an animal can be easy **prey**. Other dinosaurs such as the great *Tyrannosaurus rex* (*T. rex*) hunt *Triceratops.*

The dinosaur looks up to see a female *Triceratops.* He stands a little taller. He shows off the tall frill on his head. He's trying to impress her.

Suddenly, something crashes through the bushes. Another male *Triceratops* has arrived. He wants to attract the female too. The males get ready to fight for the **mate**.

They lunge at each other with their strong bodies. Their horns clash and lock together. The female watches. The male who first spotted her gets his chance. He jabs the other dinosaur with his front horn. The other *Triceratops* is injured,

When two male *Triceratops* fought, they usually both survived. Each *Triceratops* likely just wanted to show it was stronger than the other.

but he will heal. He walks away, defeated. The female is impressed by the winner. She chooses him for a mate.

Prehistoric Reptiles

Dinosaurs were **prehistoric** creatures that roamed Earth for about 245 million years. They were reptiles. Modern reptiles include lizards, alligators, and snakes. Birds seen today are also relatives of some dinosaurs.

Dinosaurs are extinct. This means they no longer exist. Dinosaurs went extinct about

Dangerous Mating

Some *Triceratops* bones show evidence that they fought and hurt each other. These injuries could have happened at any time. But after studying modern reptiles and birds, scientists believe that mating season was most likely when the dinosaurs fought.

Some reptiles today, such as the frilled lizard, also have frills.

66 million years ago. Paleontologists are scientists who study **fossils** of plants and animals. They have discovered about 700 kinds of dinosaurs.

Barnum Brown was a paleontologist. He worked with the fossils of a *Triceratops* found in Hell Creek, Montana.

Paleontologists have studied *Triceratops.* They know a lot about this type of dinosaur. That's because *Triceratops* fossils are some of the most commonly found dinosaur fossils.

Paleontologists believe that *Triceratops* once lived in modern-day western North America about 69 million years ago. Many fossils have been found in the state of Montana. These fossils have provided a lot of information about the dinosaur.

Further Evidence

Look at the website below. Does it give any new evidence to support Chapter One?

Triceratops

abdocorelibrary.com/triceratops

Scientists believe that many *Triceratops* lived in swampy areas near water.

GENTLE GIANTS

Triceratops was big and strong. This dinosaur was similar to an African elephant in size. It moved slowly. But it didn't have to hunt. *Triceratops* was a herbivore. It ate only plants. The dinosaur had a powerful beak-like mouth.

The biggest *Triceratops* fossil yet found is nicknamed Big John. Scientists think the dinosaur died from an injury to its frill.

With strong jaws and sharp teeth, *Triceratops* could grind and shred its food. It could eat food that other dinosaurs couldn't, such as tough plants.

Triceratops had a large head. It took up about one-third of the dinosaur's body.

The biggest skull paleontologists have found was about 8.2 feet (2.5 m) long.

Triceratops had three horns on its head. One was above the mouth and nose, and two more were above the eyes. The word *Triceratops* means "three-horned face" in Latin. *Triceratops* used its horns for protection.

Growing Horns

Triceratops horns changed in shape and size as the dinosaur got older. When *Triceratops* was young, the horns above its eyes were short and straight. As it got older, those horns curved backward. Its horns curved forward when *Triceratops* became an adult.

Another key feature of *Triceratops* was something called a frill. The frill looked like a big fan on the back of its head. Scientists think the frill was used to impress mates. It could also be used to protect the dinosaur from **predators**. A bigger frill could also show that a *Triceratops* was older. The dinosaur's frill got bigger with age.

As Big as a Bus

Triceratops could weigh more than 11,000 pounds (5,000 kg). Some even weighed up to 15,750 pounds (7,140 kg). *Triceratops* had four short, wide legs to support all that weight. These beasts walked on all fours, unlike dinosaurs such as *T. rex*.

How Heavy?

A large *Triceratops* would have weighed more than a large African elephant.

New discoveries show that dinosaurs might have had patterned skin. They also may have been more brightly colored than scientists originally thought.

Triceratops could grow up to 30 feet (9 m) long. That is the length of an average school bus! Some of that length was from its tail.

PRIMARY SOURCE

Triceratops used its horns to protect itself. Evidence can be found on fossils. The Natural History Museum in London wrote,

> A partial *Triceratops* fossil . . . has a horn that was bitten off. . . . The fossil shows that the horn healed after being bitten, so at least some *Triceratops* survived [fights].

Source: *"Triceratops." Natural History Museum*, n.d., nhm.ac.uk. Accessed 4 May 2023.

Comparing Texts

Think about the quote. Does it support the information in this chapter? Or does it give a different perspective? Explain how in a few sentences.

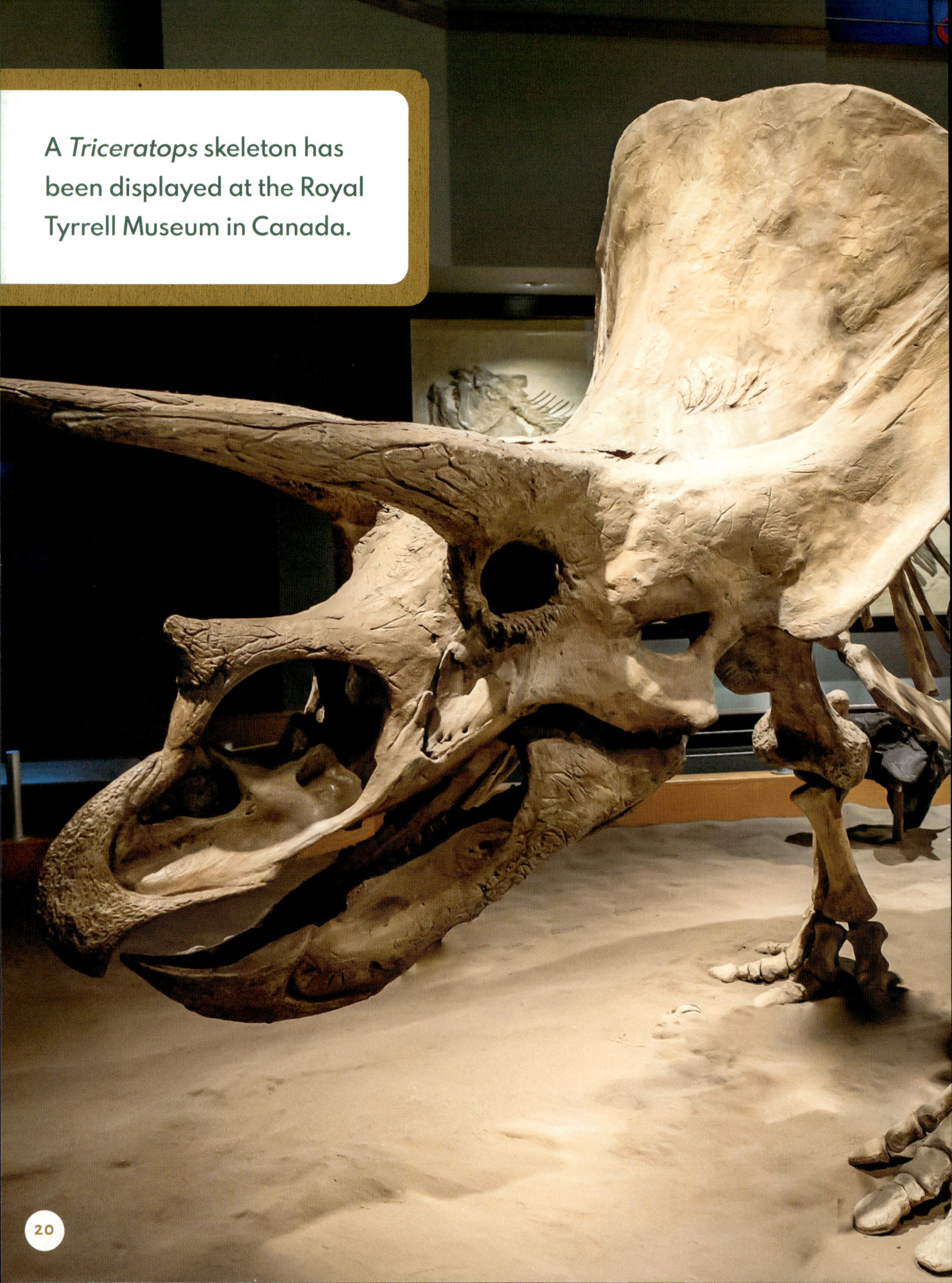

A *Triceratops* skeleton has been displayed at the Royal Tyrrell Museum in Canada.

FOSSIL FINDINGS

Paleontologists go on digs to look for fossils. From fossils, scientists learn information about what a dinosaur looked like or how it may have behaved. Most fossils of *Triceratops* have been found in modern-day North America.

They came from Montana, South Dakota, Colorado, Wyoming, and parts of Canada.

In those areas, scientists have found parts of skeletons. Some were from babies. No complete skeletons have been discovered yet. Paleontologists have found teeth marks from *T. rex* on *Triceratops* horns and skulls. The scientists could tell that the wounds healed while the dinosaurs were alive.

The Fossils of Hell Creek

Triceratops fossils have been found in the Hell Creek formation in northeastern Montana. Paleontologists believe this site is where dinosaurs most recently roamed. That is one reason why this site has so many fossils. Scientists have found hundreds of *Triceratops* bones in Hell Creek.

Paleontologists laid out bones from a *Triceratops*'s spine while they put together the dinosaur's skeleton.

Triceratops could defend itself from predators. But sometimes, *Triceratops* did not win the fight. Other bite marks showed that some *Triceratops* were eaten by predators.

Fossils are sometimes displayed in museums after they are found. Museums Victoria in Melbourne, Australia, has the world's most complete and best-**preserved** *Triceratops*.

It was discovered in Montana in 2014 and put on display in 2021. This dinosaur is 67 million years old. The skeleton is 87 percent complete. The skull and spine are whole. The collection also includes samples of skin impressions. These show the texture of the dinosaur's skin. This *Triceratops* is one of the most important dinosaur skeletons that has ever been discovered.

A 65-million-year-old *Triceratops* is on display at the American Museum of Natural History in New York City. This dinosaur's bones have marks on them from an injury. The dinosaur may have fought with another *Triceratops.*

Fossils can be very fragile. Paleontologists must be careful when cleaning fossils.

Triceratops Today

Triceratops are shown in movies as they may have looked. One example is in *Jurassic Park*. This movie series is about dinosaur researchers.

The *Triceratops* in *Jurassic Park* is so sick that it cannot stand up. Researchers look at its eyes and mouth to figure out what is wrong.

They study living dinosaurs such as *Triceratops* in a dinosaur park.

The first movie shows a sick *Triceratops* that the researchers help. When the movie was made, scientists didn't know as much about *Triceratops* as they do now. But the dinosaur is mostly accurate in the movie. Its size and shape are correct. The *Triceratops* in the movie is a herbivore, just like the dinosaur was in real life.

However, a few parts of the *Triceratops's* looks are not as accurate. The dinosaur's head should have been bigger in the movie. The horn above its snout should have been smaller.

Triceratops once walked Earth as a mighty dinosaur. Today, scientists have shared information to help everyone learn about these dinosaurs. But there is still much more to learn.

Explore Online

Visit the website below. Does it give any new information about Triceratops that wasn't in Chapter Three?

Triceratops: Fate of the Dinosaurs

abdocorelibrary.com/triceratops

DINO DETAILS

Four short, wide legs to support a heavy body

Frill to impress mates
Three horns used for protection
Beak-like mouth that could grind and shred food

Glossary

fossil
the remains of very old animals or plants

herd
a group of animals that travel together

mate
one of two animals that breed together to create offspring

predator
an animal that hunts other animals

prehistoric
having to do with the time before written history

preserved
kept from becoming damaged or wearing out

prey
an animal that is food for a predator

Online Resources

To learn more about *Triceratops*, visit our free resource websites below.

Visit **abdocorelibrary.com** or scan this QR code for free Common Core resources for teachers and students, including vetted activities, multimedia, and booklinks, for deeper subject comprehension.

Visit **abdobooklinks.com** or scan this QR code for free additional online weblinks for further learning. These links are routinely monitored and updated to provide the most current information available.

Learn More

An, Priscilla. *Brachiosaurus*. Abdo, 2024.

Chinsamy-Turan, Anusuya. *Dinosaurs and Other Prehistoric Life*. DK, 2021.

Hulick, Kathryn. *Dinosaurs*. Abdo, 2023.

Index

About the Author

Steph Giedd is a former high school English teacher who now works as an editor. Originally from southern Iowa, Giedd now lives in Minneapolis, Minnesota, with her husband, daughter, and pets.